Buddhism for Beginners

How to Practice Buddhism to Cultivate Happiness and Live a Stress-Free Life

Grace Bell

© **Text Copyright 2019 by Grace Bell - All rights reserved.**

This document is geared towards providing exact and reliable information in regards to the topic and issue covered. The publication is sold with the idea that the publisher is not required to render accounting, officially permitted, or otherwise, qualified services. If advice is necessary, legal or professional, a practiced individual in the profession should be ordered.

From a Declaration of Principles which was accepted and approved equally by a Committee of the American Bar Association and a Committee of Publishers and Associations.

In no way is it legal to reproduce, duplicate, or transmit any part of this document in either electronic means or in printed format. Recording of this publication is strictly prohibited and any storage of this document is not allowed unless with written permission from the publisher. All rights reserved.

The information provided herein is stated to be truthful and consistent, in that any liability, in terms of inattention or otherwise, by any usage or abuse of any policies, processes, or directions contained within is the solitary and utter responsibility of the recipient reader. Under no circumstances will any legal responsibility or blame be held against the publisher for any reparation, damages, or monetary loss due to the information herein, either directly or indirectly.

Respective authors own all copyrights not held by the publisher.

The information herein is offered for informational purposes solely, and is universal as so. The presentation of the information is without contract or any type of guarantee assurance.

The trademarks that are used are without any consent, and the publication of the trademark is without permission or backing by the trademark owner. All trademarks and brands within this book are for clarifying purposes only and are owned by the owners themselves, not affiliated with this document.

Paperback ISBN: 978-1-951548-48-3

Table of Contents

Introduction 1

Chapter 1: Buddhism, Explained 3
A Brief History 3
Why Choose Buddhism? 4

Chapter 2: Grasping the Teachings of Buddhism 6
The Four Noble Truths 6
The Noble Eightfold Path 8
Points to Remember 9

Chapter 3: The Benefits of Buddhism on Stress and Anxiety 10
Buddha's Approach to Stress and Anxiety 11
Dealing With Stress Through Buddhism: Is It Possible? ... 12

Chapter 4: Buddhist Exercises and Practices That Combat Stress 13
Mindfulness Meditation 14
A Simple Mindfulness Meditation 18
Other Buddhist Meditations.. 19

Chapter 5: The Pursuit of Happiness 21
Understanding Suffering 22
Cultivating Real Happiness 24

Conclusion 26

Check Out My Other Books 28

Introduction

Buddhism is a faith and spirituality that has seen a resurgence from time to time during our history. This is because its beliefs, traditions, and spiritual practices seem to resonate with the masses when they are feeling lost, or in need of guidance. Also, with Buddhism, people don't feel bogged down by dogma and religious fanaticism, which really gives them the freedom to practice Buddhism in the way that best suits them.

Let this not be taken to mean, though, that Buddhism is a loose faith, allowing individuals to cherry pick those parts of it that work for them while ignoring the others. This is certainly not that case. Buddhism, instead, offers a variety of approaches to the teachings and spiritual practices as laid out by the Buddha. It is, therefore, more accurate to say that with Buddhism, you will have a number of choices regarding the particular school you want to follow.

But, just what is Buddhism? Can it really lead you on the path to enlightenment and liberation, even happiness? What benefits do practitioners of Buddhism enjoy, and can you too, as a layman, enjoy the very same? These are just some of the questions that will be addressed in this book, with the goal of introducing you to this form of spirituality, and leaving you to make up your mind for yourself whether or not Buddhism is for you.

Chapter 1: Buddhism, Explained

"You only lose what you cling to."
— Gautama Buddha

Let us address a basic question that is probably on your mind right now. Just what is Buddhism?

Buddhism can best be described as a religion. It has tenets and practices that must be adhered to if one is to experience enlightenment and liberation. Enlightenment is believed to be the end goal, much like Heaven is the end goal for Christians. Rebirth and Karma are core beliefs in Buddhism. As are The Four Noble Truths and The Noble Eightfold Path. These beliefs will be explained a little later.

We all know that Christianity started with Jesus Christ and Islam with the prophet Muhammed. Likewise, Buddhism is based on the teachings of the Buddha, and the following short subsection will give you a brief history of this faith.

A Brief History

Siddhartha Gautama was the original Buddha or enlightened one. After observing all the suffering around him, through meditation and deep analysis, he sought an antidote. He managed to achieve a state of enlightenment, marking the end of attachments and suffering, releasing him from the cycle of rebirth upon his death!

While Buddhism has been through many modifications and metamorphoses in its 2500-year history, there are currently three distinct branches. These are, namely, the **Great Vehicle**, the **Diamond Vehicle**, and the **Doctrine of the Elders**. Despite these three distinct branches, all the teachings of this faith, founded around the 5th century in India (the part that is modern day Nepal) are based on the teachings of the

Buddha, summarized as the **Four Noble Truths** and the **Eightfold Path**.

Explanations of these doctrines will follow in the next chapter. For now, though, let us answer another question that is probably nagging at you. And that is, why should you choose Buddhism over any of the myriad other religions and faiths available today?

Why Choose Buddhism?

People are drawn to Buddhism for a number of reasons, the most notable being that they are seeking real solutions to the problems they face on a daily basis. While it is true that we are all individuals, and therefore we tend to think our circumstances and responses to these circumstances are unique to us. This is and isn't true. While the nature of your problems, the people involved and places in which these problems occur, most of us really are experiencing various versions of the same problems.

We have problems in our relationships, problems with anger that leads very often to disputes and even physical fights, problems at work, in our home life, economic problems, wars, and terrorism. These are real problems that require real solutions, and while Buddhism doesn't claim to solve these problems, it certainly **puts them into perspective!**

Buddhism has a very rational foundation, which makes it very attractive to rational thinkers. It doesn't encourage blind faith, but instead uses logic and reason to lay out a path to enlightenment, one that will lead you to calm and inner peace. This will come from understanding the nature of suffering, accepting and knowing your place in the world, and dealing with the real problems you face pragmatically.

Finally, Buddhism is in no way idealistic. It doesn't aim to paint pretty pictures that lull you into a false sense of security. It emphasizes reality, bringing you up close and personal with the reality of the world we occupy and showing you how to navigate this world with a deep calm found nowhere else!

What makes Buddhism different from the many eastern religions out there, you ask? It is the foundation upon which it is based. The **Four Noble Truths** and the **Eightfold Path** are discussed in the next chapter.

Chapter 2: Grasping the Teachings of Buddhism

"Attachment leads to suffering."
— Gautama Buddha

As stated previously, Buddhism has undergone many variations in the last 2500 years. However, the basic doctrines remain constant, forming the glue, if you will, that keeps Buddhists and Buddhism easily recognizable.

These **doctrines** are:
- The Four Noble Truths
- The Eightfold Path

Buddhism has, as its primary focus, the description of reality as processes and relations, rather than substance or entity. There are also **five aggregates** used to analyze experience. These are **material existence, sensations, perceptions, psychic constructs, and consciousness**.

The following is a short, concise description of the Four Noble Truths. This in no way serves to indoctrinate you to the Buddhist way. It is simply to give you a working knowledge of these **Truths**, and also the **Eightfold Path**, so that you can make up your own mind whether or not this is something you would like to explore.

The Four Noble Truths

The Four Noble Truths is a teaching from Buddha's first sermon after his enlightenment. These truths include the existence of suffering (dukkah), the reason for suffering (samudaya), ending suffering (nirhodha), and becoming free from suffering (magga). Here is what each truth entails:

Truth #1–suffering's existence (dukkah)

This First Noble Truth recognizes that suffering is a reality of humanity. It recognizes that the reality of suffering is also temporary and conditional on account of being compounded by other factors. The Pali word dukkah is itself translated to mean 'temporary.' Suffering, therefore, is not just what happens when something traditionally considered 'bad' happens. In fact, even that which is considered enjoyable, valuable, and precious, is temporary as it too will end. This first noble truth (the reality of suffering) brings us to the next truth–why we suffer.

Truth #2–why suffering happens (samudaya)

This, the second of the four noble truths in the teachings of Buddhism looks at why it is we suffering. Suffering, according to this truth is a result of attachments. That is, it results from cravings or 'thirst'–represented as tanha in the original language. This truth looks deeply at the fact that the human condition often seeks something outside of itself–be it physical things, ideas, opinions, belief systems, or perceptions–in an effort to gain a sense of security about who we are. Yet, no matter how much we acquire, we are never satisfied, and we grow increasingly disgruntled with the state of the world around us, and the inability of our lives to conform to these attachments and expectations we have formed. Hence, we continue to suffer. The teachings of Buddhism on rebirth/reincarnation and karma are closely related to the concepts embodied in this Second Noble Truth.

Truth #3–Ending suffering (nirhodha)

The Third Noble Truth–the end of suffering–aims to prescribe a solution for the human condition as highlighted in the first and second noble truths. The Third Noble Truth asserts that through right and diligent practice, we can alleviate suffering as we put an end to 'cravings,' desires and the attachments that result. By ending the never-ending chase after satisfaction, we become awakened and begin to put an end to our suffering. This state of being awakened is represented by the word bodhi in the original language. Beings who are awakened or enlightened exists in a state of Nirvana. Meditation is a perfect practice for beginning the journey toward the end of suffering.

Truth # 4–releasing suffering (magga)

This Fourth Noble Truth is where the rubber meets the road in the teachings of Buddhism. In Buddhism, as is often the case in many traditional western religions, merely 'believing' or identifying with a doctrine through mental assent is not enough. Instead, the emphasis is to be placed on impactful, practical action. One walks the path of enlightenment through action. The action thereof, in the teachings of Buddhism, is found in **the Noble Eightfold Path**.

The Noble Eightfold Path

The Noble Eightfold Path is seen as a further unpacking of another teaching in Buddhism known as the Threefold Way. The Noble Eightfold path highlights eight areas of 'right' or 'perfect' practice. All these eight practices are intertwined and connected to each other. None of the eight practices exist on its own.

1. Right View
2. Right Resolve
3. Right Speech
4. Right Action
5. Right Livelihood
6. Right Effort
7. Right Mindfulness, and
8. Right Concentration

Points to Remember

These are the core beliefs of doctrines that govern the Buddhist's life. The teachings of Buddhism are both simple and complex at the same time. These teachings look at the multi-tiered reality of the human condition—namely suffering—and then provides the solutions through right practice.

It is easy to see how acceptance of the **Four Noble Truths**, and subsequently, an earnest endeavor to follow the **Eightfold Path**, can lead you to inner peace and calm, despite the often tumultuous experiences of your daily life. But, in the absence of commitment to this faith in its entirety, can you still reap the rewards offered by the Buddhist lifestyle? Can you extract from Buddhism the tools needed to cope effectively with stress and anxiety, for example?

The next chapter discusses just this question.

Chapter 3: The Benefits of Buddhism on Stress and Anxiety

*"Greater in battle
than the man who would conquer
a thousand-thousand men,
is he who would conquer
just one —
himself.
Better to conquer yourself
than others.
When you've trained yourself,
living in constant self-control,
neither a deva nor gandhabba,
nor a Mara banded with Brahmas,
could turn that triumph
back into defeat."*
— Gautama Buddha

Being an adult is hard work. How many of you haven't had days when you wished you were five-years-old again, without a care in the world? The truth of the matter is, though, that we grow up, and with growing up comes increased responsibility, loans, mortgages, car notes, utilities, once contract after the other, health insurance, and credit card debt!

You can probably think of many others to add to this list. And as your list grows, the more overwhelmed you feel. Stress, anxiety, and panic have really become such an integral part of our society and culture that a lot of us fool ourselves into thinking that **we actually work well under pressure.** This isn't necessarily always true, though, and stress and anxiety really have the ability to paralyze you.

So what can you do to rid yourself of stress and anxiety? The truth is, **nothing**. Stress is a part of life that cannot be avoided. The best you can hope to do is to learn ways to better deal with stress and anxiety when they crop up. Let us see now, what Buddhism says about these two demons that really have the nasty habit of knocking the wind out of your sails!

Buddha's Approach to Stress and Anxiety

Just over 2500 years ago, Buddha referenced the **monkey mind**! What on earth was he talking about?

Buddha was here referring to that universal condition, suffered by all human beings to one degree or another, where we think that our situation is unique and that all the crazy chaos going on in our heads is out of our control!

Life has really not changed too much in the time between the 5th century BC and the twenty-first century AD. Much like today, folks were dealing with increases in wealth, astonishingly rapid advances in technology, stability in their lives and careers rocked by constant change, destructive warfare, economic turmoil, and disruption to set patterns of life that were really widespread.

However, through all of this, The Buddha managed, not without effort, to uncover a path to true and lasting happiness. Methodically, step-by-step, he trained his mind in order to achieve contentment. And contentment, no matter how you look at it, will always be the surest way to keep stress and anxiety in check!

Are these tools and training available to you today? Of course, they are. Through his own personal experience, through his journey on his path to enlightenment, the Buddha has left us with practical steps that we can use today in order for us to achieve this state of contentment. The following subsection will let you know how, through the teachings of Buddhism, you can do just that.

The practicality of these steps will really leave you wondering why this stuff isn't taught in schools!

Dealing With Stress Through Buddhism: Is It Possible?

It most certainly is possible to handle stress and anxiety with the tools and methods taught by Buddhists. They have been practicing these for thousands of years, and they are as relevant today as they were in the fifth century. We have seen that the conditions under which stress is created are no different today than they were two thousand years ago. And so, it stands to reason, that help has been available to us for just as long.

Buddhist wisdom makes reference to a central quality to our suffering. He further references a central **cure**, if you will. There is no reason why this cure cannot be applied to stress and anxiety, which are themselves forms of suffering!

You will notice recurring themes when you look at your anxiety and stress levels. Therein lies the secret to relieving your stress and better managing your anxiety, according to Buddhism. All you need to do, instead of fleeing from the triggers and causes of stress, which is the most natural response, face them head on, through **mindfulness** and **meditation**. Your mind is the most powerful tool you have at your disposal when dealing with stress, and its ugly stepsisters, panic, and anxiety.

The following chapter will discuss in detail **how you can use mindfulness and meditation to combat stress!**

Chapter 4: Buddhist Exercises and Practices That Combat Stress

"No one saves us but ourselves. No one can and no one may. We ourselves must walk the path."
— Gautama Buddha

Meditation is a buzz word that has been doing the rounds for thousands of years now. There are so many types of meditation that it is really quite easy to become bogged down in the details, unable to choose they type of meditation practice to suit your needs. Buddhism offers you a variety of options too, and depending on your lifestyle and the time you have to practice this, it is easy to find a suitable form of meditation for your requirements.

To combat stress successfully, and to manage your anxiety so that it no longer cripples you, are the main focus of your meditative efforts. Buddha, at a time when the world really was in turmoil, managed to still his mind and discover a path to happiness and contentment that would otherwise have passed him right by had he not mastered his mind. You too will need to gain mastery of your mind, learn to empty your mind, to quiet your mind, if you are to have any hope of succeeding in your efforts.

Meditation needs not be regimented. At least, that is certainly not the way with Buddhist meditation. It focuses on the process, and not just the potential outcomes. The reason for this, at least one of them, is that everyone's path is different, and everyone responds differently to the process of meditation. Some people take to the practice quickly, almost effortlessly, like a duck to water. Other people have a more difficult time about it, unable to concentrate long enough to really get into it.

And therein lies the mistake many people make when they start meditating. People think that they need to concentrate on the act to reap the rewards!

One of the principal forms of Buddhist meditation is called mindfulness meditation. It is probably the most powerful form of meditation because it focuses on training the mind, which central to the practice of Buddhism. The path to enlightenment is closely attached to a letting go of all clinginess. Clinginess and attachment a central to suffering, and so it is imperative that you rid yourself of these traits, even if only for short bursts at a time.

Let us now discuss mindfulness meditation, and give you a basic mindfulness exercise to get you started on your path to enlightenment!

Mindfulness Meditation

It is certainly possible to practice mindfulness without being a practicing Buddhist. However, it is impossible to be a true Buddhist without mindfulness!

The three overarching purposes of mindfulness meditation give an indication as to why this is the case. ***These purposes are:***

- ***Knowing Your Mind***
- ***Training Your Mind, and***
- ***Freeing Your Mind***

Knowing the mind is a process of simple discovery. Take notice of who you are, your mind, body, and your emotions. This knowing is a very conscious effort too, supported in a great part by stillness. This stillness highlights what is really going on in your mind, and while you focus just knowing, you should make no attempts at changing anything. All you do in this part of the process is to observe!

Training the mind is made possible by the fact that the mind is pliable and malleable. Because your mind is not static, it is important that you take full responsibility for it, or risk it being shaped by external forces. Start with simple things, like training your mind on compassion and kindness. Mindfulness often reveals internal conflicts as well as conflicts with others, and you cannot resolve conflicts with further conflicts. This will only add to your suffering.

You need to train your mind to accept things as they are. Instead of trying to organize the world around you, focus on training your mind to stay calm and relaxed no matter what is happening around you. This will help in the development of better concentration, and stability of the mind. Discernment, courage, ethical virtues, and generosity are other aspects and qualities that your mind can be trained at developing.

You will find it easier to choose one particular area of focus, and once you have made progress you can move on to the next one.

Freeing the mind is the third purpose of mindfulness, and it is probably the most important. This is because once you have freed your mind, you will have developed your capacity to release clinginess. This is a long process, usually undertaken in small increments, each small step bringing its own benefits. You must know this in advance, though, that the attainment of this freedom will come at great cost, and will require significant training and knowledge. Much like your body needs to be taken care of daily, so too does your mind need regular exercise and care.

Now that you understand the **threefold purposes of mindfulness**, let us get into the practicalities of mindfulness meditation. When you understand too, that **mindfulness is all about paying attention, on purpose, in the moment, nonjudgmentally**, then you will be equipped for this particular practice. Remember, mindfulness isn't forced, and it isn't focused on anything other than the present moment. It is about ***being continuously present, with experience, with the gentlest effort!***

Paying attention on purpose means more than just a vague habitual awareness of your thoughts. Much like eating, where you can be aware of what you're doing, your mind in a hundred different places, though, the same can be said of your thoughts. So, the fact that you are slightly aware of your thoughts, they tend to wander in a million different directions. You start to actively shape your mind when you focus on your experience with purpose!

When you pay attention in the moment, you understand that you only have the **present moment**! The past has happened, it is gone, and there is nothing that you can do to get back any lost moments. The future has really not happened. It is really just an illusion of dream and hopes, plans and intentions that have not happened until they do. This is not to say that you cannot think about the past or the future, but just that your concern is always about what is going on right now.

Focusing on the **now** becomes an anchor for you, creating a fertile environment in your mind where calm, freedom, and contentment can grow!

Finally, paying attention nonjudgmentally means that you approach your thoughts and emotions with equanimity. This means that while you are cognitively aware that some experiences are pleasant, others are not, you do not react to these perceptions of the experiences. On an emotional level, you don't react, approaching these experiences instead with a sense of balance, and stillness.

The purposes of mindfulness have been explained. How you should pay attention has also been explained. Before we move on to an actual mindfulness meditation, it is important to discuss briefly the Buddha's **Four Foundations Of Mindfulness**. It is important that you understand these if you are to meditate mindfully.

The Foundations are:

- The First Foundation comes from knowing what any experience actually feels like in your body
- The Second Foundation is noting the feeling tones-the pleasant, the unpleasant, and the neutral-that accompany every moment's experience
- The Third Foundation is to bear witness to and be aware of your emotions and mental state in the moment
- The Fourth Foundation is being open to the impersonal truth about life as revealed in the present moment

So, just how do you go about a session in mindfulness meditation?

A Simple Mindfulness Meditation

First, you consciously choose to concentrate on your breath. A focus on your breathing makes you immediately aware of your mind's tendency to wander. This discipline brings you to the present moment, developing in you an alert sensitivity and awareness that is, in its most basic form, what mindfulness is.

Without thinking too much about how you are breathing, just keeping your attention the natural flow of air in and out of your nose, filling your chest, and then going out of you. Your mind will wander. This is to be expected. Just notice when this happens, and bring your concentration back to your breathing. With enough practice, you will soon find yourself able to slip in and out of that **intense state of meditative absorption known as dhyana!**

Mindfulness meditation has four progressive stages. Five minutes spent on each stage is a good entry level period of practice. The **Four Stages Of Mindfulness Meditation are:**

1. You have learned to focus on your breathing now. During the first stage, you need to increase this focus by counting. On the out-breath, *count one*. Then breathe in, and *count two* as you exhale. Repeat this until your reach ten, and then start at one again. Repeat this stage for five minutes, remembering not to concentrate on how you are breathing, just focusing on the fact that you are!

2. A subtle shift in where you breathe takes place during the second stage. Unlike the first stage, where you counted on each exhalation, this time, you count on every inhalation. One, two, three, up ten, repeating this for five minutes. You focus on anticipating the coming breath now, instead of the release of the breath!

3. The third stage is about dropping the counting. Just watch every breath coming in and going out of you, with no real intention but to keep doing this for five minutes. Avoid the

temptation to keep counting. Avoid the temptation to get up and check that you did turn the stove off, or whether you locked the front door. Just breathe, easy and relaxed, focusing on nothing else but your breathing.

4. In the fourth and final stage, narrow and sharpen your concentration. There is a subtle sensation on the tip of your nose that happens every time you breathe in, and every time you breathe out. Pay attention to this sensation as each breath enters your body through your nose, and then concentrate on this sensation as your breath leaves your body, again through your nose. Focus on this sensation for five minutes, and then slowly bring yourself into a state of awareness.

And this is how you practice mindfulness meditation. The length of time can be slowly built up until pretty soon you will be able to practice this fundamental form of meditation for a full hour without any significant lapses in concentration. You will also find that you can also practice it anywhere, as your ability to drown out the distractions of life easier. The benefits of this kind of meditating, and others outlined below, need no further mention now. Just know that you will gain incredible peace and calm, and you will be able to handle stress and anxiety better!

Other Buddhist Meditations

Focused Attention Meditation is not dissimilar, in theory at least, to mindfulness meditation. For the duration of the meditation session, you keep your attention on a single object. This object can be visualization or a mantra, or it can be a physical object like a part of your body or an external object like a candle or a vase. ***Samatha*** is a form of focused attention meditation that is extremely popular in Buddhism.

Open Monitoring Meditation is the opposite of Focused Attention! Instead of one particular object, you leave your mind open. You monitor every aspect of the experience, in the absence of any sort of attachment or judgment. You simply see all internal and external perceptions exactly for what they are. During this process, you simply monitor the context and content of the moments as the float by, without reacting to these moments or becoming emotionally involved in them.

Finally, *Effortless Presence Meditation* is a form of Zen meditation that requires no external object. You just sit still, aware of what is going on in your head, observing these thoughts without harping on any one in particular. Just makes sure that you sit with your back completely straight!

There are of course hundreds if not thousands of other Buddhist meditations that you can try. Find one that resonates with you, one that you can practice easily, and you will soon find that apart from just reducing and better-managing stress and anxiety, you will also find yourself a lot happier.

The last chapter will discuss the influence of ***Buddhism and its practice can lead to real happiness!***

Chapter 5: The Pursuit of Happiness

Piti is a word from early ***Pali*** texts for ***happiness***. Translated, it means ***rapture or deep tranquility***! It is important that you understand ***piti*** if you are to grasp the Buddha's teachings on the subject.

As Buddha explained, emotional and physical feelings attach or correspond to objects. In much the same way that hearing happens when a sense organ (the ear) and a sense object (sound) come into contact, so too is happiness created as a result of certain objects, such as the birth of a child, or getting that dress you've been saving for.

The trouble with happiness, though, comes in the longevity, or lack thereof, of the objects associated with this state. Happy events are soon followed by unhappy ones, a child becomes sick soon after it is born, or your new dress soon becomes worn and dated. So the attachment of happiness to these objects is never a permanent solution!

True happiness, as a feature of enlightenment, has no foundation in objects, therefore. It is based solidly on mental discipline and therefore is more lasting than its transient counterpart. If you have truly cultivated ***Piti***, then you will appreciate the impermanence of transitory emotions. You will find yourself continually reaching for things that you actually want in your life, letting the things you don't want go.

According to Buddha too, enlightenment does not lead to happiness. Rather, cultivating a state of happiness is essential to realize enlightenment. However, to know true happiness, you must understand its counterpart. All the suffering in the world leads to unhappiness, and there are a lot of ways that people can and do suffer today. Understanding suffering, therefore, is essential if you are to cultivate a genuine state of happiness.

Let us now briefly discuss suffering.

Understanding Suffering

Suffering is an unavoidable fact of life. Birth, old age, sickness, and death are four unavoidable physical sufferings. The frustration of desire, contact with people you don't like, and being separated from people you care about are three forms of mental suffering that are also unavoidable. While the focus of the bulk of Buddha's teachings was centered ending suffering, he understood that people need firstly to accept that suffering was a part of life.

Physical suffering is the most tangible form of suffering. You know when you are in pain, when your eyesight and hearing start to fade, or when your teeth are suddenly so brittle that it becomes difficult to eat. When you are faced with illness and disease, you are chronically aware of the pain and discomfort. The pain of death is the same, from the physical to the grief and suffering. Even something as beautiful as childbirth brings incredible pain to the mother, and a lot of distress to the child.

You might not be suffering physically right now, and as a result, you could be very complacent. It is so easy for people to believe that they will never get sick, be in an accident, get old, break an arm or leg, or experience any of the other ailments that other people seem to be too prone to. When you are well, or young, it is all too easy to think that you are not, every day, aging a little bit more. The fundamental truth of the matter is this, no matter how healthy you are right now, or whether or not you live most of your life in relatively good health, you will eventually get old, get sick, and die.

Another basic truth about this type of suffering is that it cannot be shared, and must be born alone. Regardless of the nature, whether it is just a common cold, a minor injury such as a sprained ankle, a major injury such as a broken leg, or even a sad event, you cannot exchange your suffering with other people. Only you alone can experience what this suffering feels like for you.

Mental suffering also affects the individual more than it does groups of people. This is because people are just that, individuals, with individual responses that are unique to the personal makeup and set of circumstances. So again, as with physical suffering, you have no choice but to take ownership of this suffering, and deal with it on your own. That is not to say that you cannot call on support, but ultimately, the buck will stop with you.

This form of suffering takes on many forms. Sadness, loneliness, depression are all just some of the masks worn by mental suffering. Loss or separation from loved ones, either through moving or death, are other faces. That unpleasant feeling you get when you are faced with people you don't like is another still. And also the inability to satisfy the many wants and needs that we have adds yet another face.

Different forms of mental suffering affect us at the various stages of our lives, too. As a baby, you cry because you cannot articulate your needs and wants. Teenagers feel slighted by being denied a late-night outing by their parents. Adults feel frustration with being unable to pay bills, or they may experience the frustration of an unfulfilling or complicated relationship. All these are but examples of what Buddhists collectively call mental suffering.

Now that you understand mental and physical suffering, let us take a look at how, despite this suffering, you can experience happiness.

Cultivating Real Happiness

Now you have the root of suffering, and you understand what all the forms of suffering are. You also know that these sufferings cannot be avoided, so it is pointless even trying. What you also know, and this is the most important thing, that it is possible to cultivate happiness, true, genuine, long lasting happiness, that isn't based on one specific object that will only last as long as it does before it gives way to another, equally transient object.

How can you do this?

Quiet the mind: With all the thoughts tugging at you at any one particular time, it is quite easy to become overwhelmed. You need to learn to become still. The practice of mindfulness meditation will help greatly with this. As you proceed with this practice, you will gain mastery over your thoughts, entertaining only those that deserve your attention.

Develop Love: Thoughts of love are a surefire way of enhancing your happiness. When you wish happiness for others, and wish that they are surrounded by the causes of happiness is love. And this love flows from compassion and sympathy, which are also qualities to be cultivated in your pursuit of happiness. A wonderful thing happens when you start to cultivate these triggers for happiness; they lead to other spontaneous triggers, further increasing your feelings of joy.

The long and short of it is this, happiness comes from refraining from engaging in behavior, thinking, and speech that is destructive. These destructive thoughts can stem from a number of sources, such as anger, repulsion, lust, greed, naivety, and attachment. You need to really release yourself from these negatives.

You cannot avoid them, though, so what can you do about keeping them in check? Well, you can trigger future potential happiness by looking at everything in your life, the good and the bad, with a certain measure of dullness. Rid your mind of expectations and worry, and notice how you will already start to feel happier, just from this state of tranquility.

Focus your attention on other people, on their problems, and how these are sometimes worse than yours. Allow yourself to feel true compassion for others, and stop thinking only of yourself. This compassion will trigger happiness inside you, and also give you the strength and courage to face your own problems with a little more confidence.

You have a choice, to either exaggerate your problems or see them for what they are and let them go. You also have the choice of attaching expectations to everything that you do, which leads to worry and fear of failure. Or you can see everything as an opportunity to learn instead of as a competition.

You would do well to remember that happiness is a state of mind, resulting from a disciplined, trained mind, one that knows how to choose areas of focus that will ultimately lead to a ripple effect of happiness triggers that will sustain you on your journey through life!

Conclusion

This book has not been written as a conversion tool. It has simply served to inform you of the benefits of Buddhism. It has, clearly it is hoped, given you suitable juxtapositions to help you form a frame of reference for these benefits. You have been introduced to some of the fundamental principles of this faith, and been given insights into some of its tenets. You have been shown some of the meditative practices associated with Buddhism, and you have been shown how all of these factors come together to help you live a happier life.

Happiness doesn't come from the absence of suffering, as you have learned. It comes from understanding and accepting that suffering is a part of life, and your true happiness will come from learning to navigate life's suffering with calm and relative peace of mind. As you travel the **Eightfold Path**, after you have accepted the **Four Noble Truths**, you will come closer and closer to enlightenment, which will free you from attachment to the **things of life**, and free up your mind and heart for nobler pursuits.

We have made no promises that this is going to be easy, although, granted, it is easier for some than for others. It is suggested, therefore, that you be gentle with yourself, and take it one step at a time. There is no rush to reach any milestones of enlightenment, and since you will probably have to unlearn your conditioning before your head is ready to embark on this journey, you will really just need to go easy on yourself.

Patience and persistence are key!

As a final note, even if you are not looking for religious conversion, the benefits of Buddhism certainly merit some consideration. Even if you are just looking for alternative ways to simply be more present in your life, then read this book again. Use what you need, discard what you don't. Just breathe through the process, taking in the newness of this experience, and exhaling all the bad that no longer serves you in your life.

Buddhism is really one of the most profound ways to achieve this balanced approach to life!

Finally, I want to thank you for reading my book. If you enjoyed the book, please take the time to share your thoughts and post a review on the book retailer's website. It would be greatly appreciated!

Best wishes,
Grace Bell

Check Out My Other Books

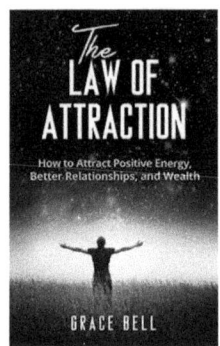

The Law of Attraction: How to Attract Positive Energy, Better Relationships, and Wealth

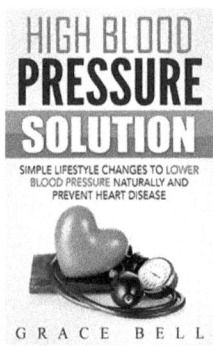

High Blood Pressure Solution: Simple Lifestyle Changes to Lower Blood Pressure Naturally and Prevent Heart Disease

Lightning Source UK Ltd.
Milton Keynes UK
UKHW021548190620
365268UK00006B/1051